Straight to the Source

Libraries and Reference Materials

John Hamilton

ABDO
Publishing Company

visit us at
www.abdopub.com

Published by ABDO Publishing Company, 4940 Viking Drive, Edina, Minnesota 55435.
Copyright © 2005 by Abdo Consulting Group, Inc. International copyrights reserved in all countries. No part of this book may be reproduced in any form without written permission from the publisher. The Checkerboard Library™ is a trademark and logo of ABDO Publishing Company.

Printed in the United States.

Cover Photo: Corbis
Interior Photos: Corbis pp. 1, 5, 6, 7, 8, 9, 10, 11, 13, 15, 17, 18, 20, 21, 23, 24, 25, 27, 29

Series Coordinator: Stephanie Hedlund
Editors: Kate A. Conley, Jennifer R. Krueger
Art Direction: Neil Klinepier

Library of Congress Cataloging-in-Publication Data

Hamilton, John, 1959-
    Libraries and reference materials / John Hamilton.
        p. cm. -- (Straight to the source)
    Summary: Describes the history of libraries, the different kinds of libraries, and the parts of a library, especially reference tools and how they can be used to do research for term papers.
    ISBN 1-59197-545-X
    1. Libraries--Juvenile literature. 2. Reference books--Juvenile literature. [1. Libraries. 2. Reference books.] I. Title.

Z665.5.H36 2004
027--dc22
                                                                        2003060485

Contents

At the Library

A library is a place where information is collected, sorted, and stored. A traditional library collects books and **periodicals**. It can also hold media such as films, DVDs, CDs, or computer **databases**.

Some of the information a library provides is in the form of reference materials. These sources may be atlases, encyclopedias, or books of **statistics**. Reference materials provide information that can be used in research papers or business reports.

However, libraries do more than simply hold information. They are a part of a community. People use libraries for research. They also go there to attend lectures, hear authors speak, or be entertained.

Libraries collect and preserve information about our society. They help us find rare books or other documents. Without libraries, we might lose the connection to our past.

At the library, people borrow books by checking them out with their library card. This is why libraries are sometimes called lending libraries.

Early Storage

The word *library* has its root in the Latin language. *Liber* is a Latin word that means "book." However, there were libraries long before books were invented. Libraries actually began as a way to store documents.

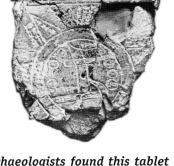

Archaeologists found this tablet in a temple in Babylonia. The temple was more than 4,500 years old.

Thousands of years ago, people made records on clay **tablets**. These records were often stored together in rooms in temples. **Archaeologists** have discovered libraries of tablets in the Middle East.

One of these ancient libraries belonged to King Ashurbanipal of

EXTRA!
Asian Libraries

As early as 403 BC, records were written on bamboo strips and silk rolls in Asia. By AD 200, libraries had grown in importance in China.

Libraries and bookmaking continued to develop in Asia. By 1234, Koreans were using movable type. This was 200 years before Europeans developed it!

Today, Asia has libraries similar to those in the United States. The National Library of China in Beijing is one of the finest libraries in the world.

Assyria. He ruled the kingdom from 668 to 627 BC. During this time, he collected about 25,000 clay **tablets**.

In ancient Greece, tablets were replaced in the 300s BC. Papyrus and **vellum** were then used to make books and scrolls. Most Greek temples had libraries that contained these early books.

The most famous ancient library was in Alexandria, Egypt. King Ptolemy I Soter started this library in the 200s BC. Hundreds of thousands of Greek documents were collected there.

The exterior of the Library of Alexandria

Romans also gathered Greek literature. Many Romans began private collections of these works. Eventually, they built libraries to house their collections.

The Roman library Bibliotheca Ulpia was established in about AD 100. It continued operating for almost 600 years. During that time, it collected most of the public records produced in Rome.

As the Roman Empire fell, many books were brought to the Imperial Library of Byzantium in Constantinople.

A Benedictine monastery library

It was planned by the Roman emperor Constantine the Great around 330. The Imperial Library preserved the literature of Greece, Rome, and **Asia Minor**.

Around 500, monasteries began collecting and copying books. The Benedictine order of monks thought it was spiritually important to read and study. Their libraries could be found all over Europe, even during the **Middle Ages**.

As time went by, Europe emerged from the **Middle Ages**. The Renaissance began in the 1200s. Art and literature were available to more people. Universities were created as centers of learning. Many of these schools had one or more libraries.

In the 1440s, middle-class people could finally afford their own book collections. Johannes Gutenberg had invented a printing press with movable type. This invention made books cheaper and easier to print.

Many personal book collections were later turned into public libraries. In France, King Charles V's private collection eventually became the Bibliothèque Nationale. Today, it is the national library of France.

The Bibliothèque Nationale was first opened to the public in 1692 as the Bibliothèque du Roi.

During the **Reformation**, many of the monastic libraries were lost. However in the 1600s, parish libraries began developing in Europe. These libraries chained the books to their cases to keep them from being stolen.

Libraries soon grew so large they needed to be organized differently. The book bays, which stood at right angles to the windows, were abandoned. Instead, bookshelves lined a room's walls. And, the books stood upright with the spine facing out.

In the 1700s, a new type of library developed. Societies started lending their collections to their members for free. Nonmembers paid a small fee, or subscription, to borrow books. These subscription libraries became popular with the public.

The concept of tax-supported libraries developed in the 1850s. These libraries provided poor students access to books for free. Today, public libraries are funded by tax money paid by the citizens they serve.

Libraries continue to bring information to the people. However, they have changed to suit the public's needs. Today's computer technology has helped libraries provide more resources.

In the late 1900s, industrialist Andrew Carnegie donated money to small communities to build free libraries. Many Carnegie libraries are still in use today.

Today's Libraries

As technology changes, so do libraries. Some libraries exist only on the Internet. However, there are also many types of libraries that you can visit in person.

The public library serves its community as a center for **literacy**. It may have complete collections of reference materials. The public library also provides entertainment, such as drummers and other acts.

One example of a public library is the New York Public Library. It first opened its doors to the public in 1911. Today, its collections total nearly 7 million books and other media. Every week, 10,000 items are added to its collections.

Another type of library is a school library. It is a good place to learn how to use a library. So, mainly elementary, middle school, and high school students use a school library.

The Boston Public Library was the first large, city library in the United States. It was founded in 1848. The library now holds more than 7 million books. More than 2 million people visit it each year.

The collections at school libraries are usually not as complete as those in public libraries. But, they often hold magazines, newspapers, and other items. Many school libraries are called media centers because of their extensive use of computers and the Internet.

Academic libraries are found in colleges and universities. They help students perform research. Most academic libraries are connected to the Internet. So, students today have the resources of many libraries at their disposal.

Special interest libraries are run by many different groups, such as museums or businesses. Some preserve rare books and manuscripts. Many special interest libraries make their collections available to the public. However, some are for members only.

Another kind of library is a national library. These libraries are created to preserve national literature. Most have a large range of materials available.

Most countries pay for and maintain a national library. These include the Bibliothèque Nationale in Paris, France, and the British Library in London, England. The Library of Congress (LOC) in Washington, D.C., is the largest national library in the world.

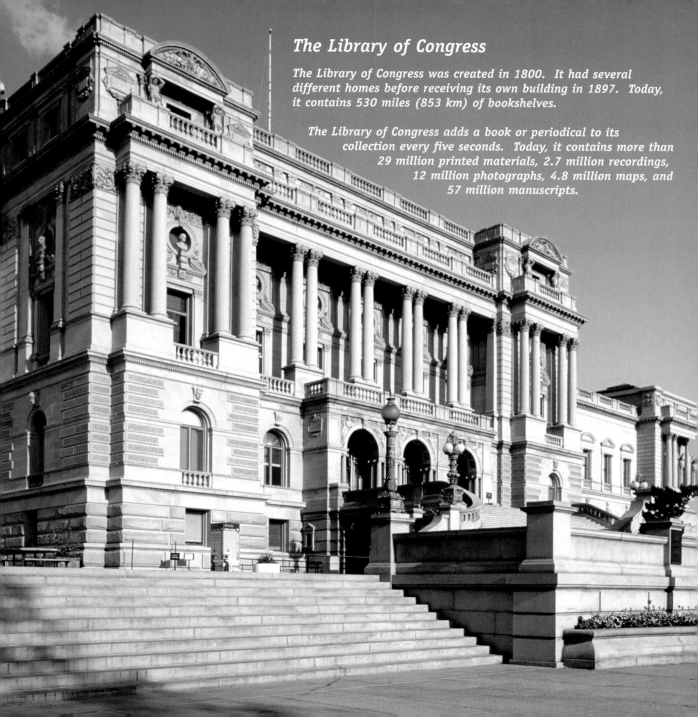

The Library of Congress

The Library of Congress was created in 1800. It had several different homes before receiving its own building in 1897. Today, it contains 530 miles (853 km) of bookshelves.

The Library of Congress adds a book or periodical to its collection every five seconds. Today, it contains more than 29 million printed materials, 2.7 million recordings, 12 million photographs, 4.8 million maps, and 57 million manuscripts.

Library Layout

Within a library, you will find several different sections. When you are looking for resources, the first place to go is the library catalog. It tells you where to find your information.

The library catalog used to be called the card catalog. It contained thousands of cards filed together in special cabinets. Each item had its own card. Today, most libraries have their catalogs on computer.

Computerized catalogs make it easy to look up a reference. Just type in a book's title, author, or subject. The computer will provide a list of books to get you started. With this list, you can find your items.

Your materials might be in the juvenile section. This section has books and magazines that are mainly of interest to children. Many juvenile sections have their own librarian. This person can help you find what you're looking for.

Another department is the adult section. The books in juvenile and adult sections are separated into two types. Fiction books are stories that come from an author's imagination. Nonfiction books are based on facts.

Computerized catalogs make it easier to search for and exchange information between libraries.

Reference books are in another department in the library. These books contain in-depth information, such as public records, atlases, or encyclopedias. Reference books can only be used while at the library. You cannot check them out.

The **periodicals** section has magazines, newspapers, **pamphlets**, and other materials that are published on a regular basis. Many libraries include years of back issues of these items on **microfiche** or in **archives**.

Reference librarians are a great resource to help you find facts for research papers.

The media center is where you can use the library's computers. You can write reports, surf the Internet, or listen to CDs. These computers also link to other libraries to find information. Copiers and **microfiche** readers are available in the media center, too.

The rows of books in any library department are referred to as open stacks. A book you want may not be in the main area of the library. It could be in a closed stack somewhere else, such as the basement. A librarian can help you retrieve such a book.

The circulation desk is where you apply for a library card. It is also where you check out or renew your materials. You can place a hold on a book or pay an overdue fine there, too. And, the librarian at the circulation desk can guide you to any section in the library.

EXTRA!

Librarians

Librarians are very organized people. They know all about collecting, storing, and retrieving documents. Finding information for the public is their most important job. So, a librarian is also known as an "information specialist."

Many librarians specialize in a certain area. Some study information science, or the best ways for society to store and use information. Others work to make sure documents are preserved.

Classification

Each section in a library contains many books and other items. It is important for a library to organize its materials. That way visitors can find what they need.

There are several systems for organizing library collections. The most famous is the Dewey decimal classification system. Libraries in more than 135 countries use this system.

Melvil Dewey

American librarian Melvil Dewey first published the Dewey decimal classification system in 1876. It divides books into ten main groups.

Each Dewey decimal group is represented by a three-digit number. The first number represents the main class. The second is the division. The third is the section. If a section needs to be even narrower, the cataloger adds a decimal followed by numbers.

Dewey Decimal Classification System

The Dewey decimal classification system starts by dividing all materials into ten main groups. From there, the numbers narrow the groups into divisions and sections.

Eventually, very specific topics are given decimals. The decimal is a pause in the digits. It makes it easier for a researcher to copy the number and find what he or she is looking for. The number after the decimal continues to be added to as needed.

For example, a book on bichons frises has a Dewey decimal classification number of 636.72.

636.72

6 = *main group of technology*
3 = *the agriculture division of technology*
6 = *the agriculture division's section of animal husbandry*
7 = *the topic of dogs*
2 = *the bichon frise breed of dogs*

Another way of categorizing books is the Library of Congress classification system. It is used at large university and research libraries. This system has more categories and room for expansion than the Dewey decimal system.

The LOC contains a huge collection of books and other media. The LOC developed its classification system in the early 1900s. About 6,000 classification numbers are added each year to keep up with new and changing topics.

The LOC classification contains a set of capital letters. The first letter represents one of 21 categories. The second letter narrows the category into a subclass.

The letters in an LOC listing are followed by numbers. The numbers allow library catalogers to narrow down a subject even more. So, librarians can be very precise by classifying books with the LOC system.

After classification, books must be cataloged. A Machine-Readable Cataloging Project (MARC II) was developed for this. MARC II uses a data format that can be read by any library's computer system. So, exchanging information between libraries is possible.

Library of Congress Classification System

The 21 main categories in the Library of Congress system are represented by letters. A second letter is added to the main category for further division. Then, numbers are added to narrow the placement even further.

For example, the book Bichons Frises has the LOC classification number SF429.B52 M87 2003.

S = main category of agriculture
F = agriculture's subdivision of animal culture
429 = book's subject of dogs
B52 = category assigned to the bichon frise breed
M87 = author information
2003 = year of publication

SF429.B52
M87
2003

Reference Books

Libraries are great sources of reference materials. These references include books, indexes, and other items that help in the research process.

Reference materials have features that assist the reader. Many reference books have entries that are organized alphabetically. Some have thumb tabs that indicate where the alphabetical list changes letters.

Dictionaries are one type of reference book. Libraries may have several different dictionaries. Some will help you find the pronunciation and meaning of words. *Merriam-Webster's* and *Oxford English Dictionary* are examples of these.

EXTRA!

Dictionary Updates

Our language constantly changes. Science and popular culture often add new words to our vocabularies. So every two to three years, groups of language experts update the dictionaries. For example, in 2001 the *Oxford English Dictionary* added Homer Simpson's catchphrase "d'oh!" as an official word.

Opposite page: *Dictionaries are arranged alphabetically. They have thumb tabs so you can quickly find the section you need.*

Another type of dictionary is a thesaurus. It is filled with **synonyms** and **antonyms** of words. The best-known is *Roget's Thesaurus*. It can help you find just the right word when you are writing a paper.

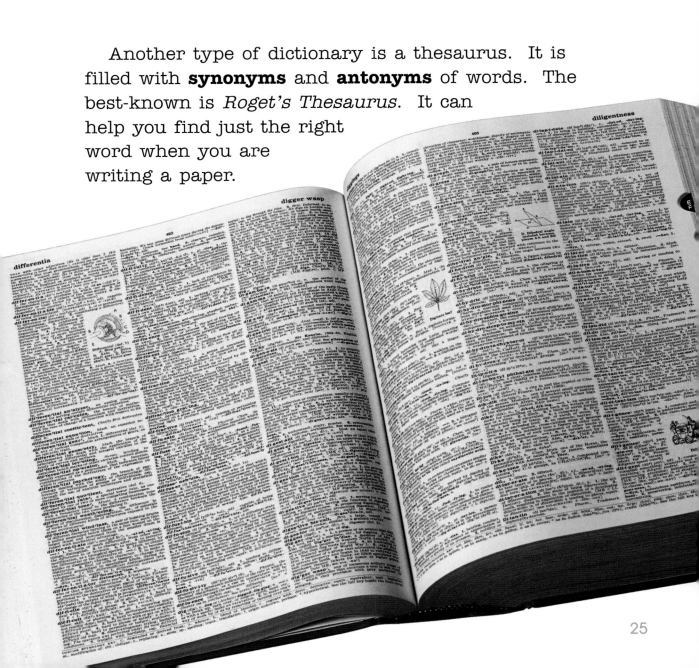

Other dictionaries include biographic and geographic information. Biographical dictionaries contain brief histories of important people. Geographic dictionaries contain information on landforms, populations, and natural resources.

Another reference book is an encyclopedia. Some encyclopedias are very general, with short articles meant for young readers. Others are meant for adults, with long, detailed articles.

An encyclopedia may be a book or a set of books. Almost all libraries own at least one set of encyclopedias. Most libraries have more.

There are many other kinds of reference materials in a library. An atlas contains a collection of maps and charts. Some atlases are very general. Others can be very specific, such as *The Early Mapping of Hawaii*.

EXTRA!

Other Types of Reference Works

There are many other reference materials in the library. Indexes guide you to materials in books, newspapers, magazines, and journals. *New York Times Index*, *Nation Newspaper Index*, and *Readers' Guide to Periodical Literature* are a few indexes.

Another reference material is a bibliography. This is a list of related publications. One example is *MLA International Bibliography*. In addition, abstracts are reference books that have summaries of journal articles and other literature.

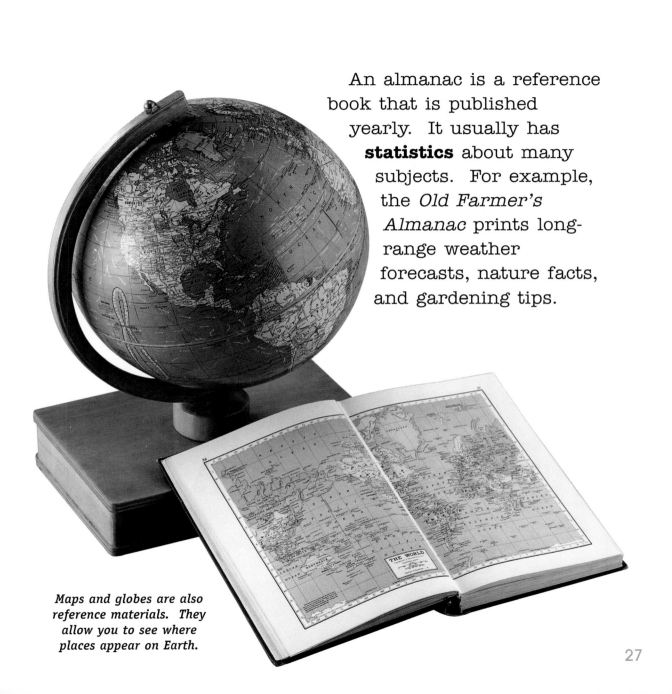

An almanac is a reference book that is published yearly. It usually has **statistics** about many subjects. For example, the *Old Farmer's Almanac* prints long-range weather forecasts, nature facts, and gardening tips.

Maps and globes are also reference materials. They allow you to see where places appear on Earth.

Using Sources

Librarians have **evaluated** the sources in the library. However, you need to evaluate research information, too. To do this, make sure hard facts support a source's statement. And, try to find the same fact in more than one reference book.

When you start writing your research paper, put the information in your own words. Don't **plagiarize** by copying a book or other source. Instead, paraphrase by summarizing the article in your own words. But, you still need to give credit to the idea's owner.

When you're done, don't forget to cite your sources. This means writing down the authors and the article names at the end of your paper. The *MLA Handbook for Writers of Research Papers* is a good source for citation.

Libraries are filled with all sorts of specialized information. To track down the information you need, use planning, imagination, and a little help from your librarian.

Research is best done at a library. Computers, reference books, and help are available there.

Glossary

antonym - a word that is opposite in meaning of the word being looked up.

archaeologist - one who studies the remains of people and activities from ancient times.

archives - organized records.

Asia Minor - the peninsula between Europe and western Asia.

database - a large collection of information.

evaluate - to determine the meaning or importance of something.

literacy - the state of being able to read and write.

microfiche - a sheet of film that contains reduced images of printed materials such as magazines. Microfiche must be read on a special machine that magnifies the images.

Middle Ages - a period from about AD 500 to 1500 characterized by a lack of education, the loss of artistic and technical skills, population decrease, and primitive economic life.

pamphlet - a printed publication without a cover.

periodical - an item that is published at a fixed period of time.

plagiarism - using someone else's words or ideas without giving him or her credit.

Reformation - a religious movement in the 1500s. People who wanted to reform the Catholic Church formed Protestantism by making these changes.

statistics - a science that deals with collecting, analyzing, and presenting numerical data.

synonym - a word that is similar in meaning to the word being looked up.

tablet - a flat slab that is suitable for writing on.

vellum - a skin of a lamb, goat, or calf prepared for writing on.

antonym - AN-tuh-nihm
archaeologist - ahr-kee-AH-luh-jihst
Ashurbanipal - ahsh-oor-BAHN-ee-pahl
Byzantium - buh-ZAN-shuhm
microfiche - MEYE-kroh-feesh
papyrus - puh-PEYE-ruhs
plagiarism - PLAY-juh-rih-zuhm
Ptolemy I Soter - TAHL-uh-mee SOHT-uhr
Renaissance - reh-nuh-SAHNS
synonym - SIH-nuh-nihm

To learn more about libraries and reference materials, visit ABDO Publishing Company on the World Wide Web at **www.abdopub.com**. Web sites about libraries are featured on our Book Links page. These links are routinely monitored and updated to provide the most current information available.

Index